W9-CIM-129

Should
STUDENT-ATHLETES
Be Paid?

By Anna Collins

Published in 2021 by
KidHaven Publishing, an Imprint of Greenhaven Publishing, LLC
353 3rd Avenue
Suite 255
New York, NY 10010

Designer: Deanna Paternostro
Editor: Jennifer Lombardo

Photo credits: Cover Mark Fann/Shutterstock.com; pp. 5 (main), 7 (top and bottom), 21 (inset, left) Aspen Photo/Shutterstock.com; p. 5 (inset) Jonathan Weiss/Shutterstock.com; p. 9 Rido/ Shutterstock.com; p. 11 Syda Productions/Shutterstock.com; p. 13 Mike Ehrmann/Getty Images; p. 15 fizkes/Shutterstock.com; p. 17 Ezra Shaw/Getty Images; p. 19 Debby Wong/Shutterstock.com; p. 21 (notepad) ESB Professional/Shutterstock.com; p. 21 (markers) Kucher Serhii/Shutterstock.com; p. 21 (photo frame) FARBAI/iStock/Thinkstock; p. 21 (inset, middle) Flamingo Images/ Shutterstock.com; p. 21 (inset, right) Mike Broglio/Shutterstock.com.

Library of Congress Cataloging-in-Publication Data

Names: Collins, Anna, author.
Title: Should student-athletes be paid? / Anna Collins.
Description: First edition. | New York : KidHaven Publishing, [2021] |
   Series: Points of view | Includes index.
Identifiers: LCCN 2019049069 (print) | LCCN 2019049070 (ebook) | ISBN
   9781534534223 (library binding) | ISBN 9781534534209 (paperback) | ISBN
   9781534534230 (ebook) | ISBN 9781534534216 (set)
Subjects: LCSH: College athletes–Economic conditions–Juvenile literature.
   | College sports–Economic aspects–Juvenile literature. | Universities
   and colleges–Economic aspects–Juvenile literature.
Classification: LCC GV351 .C655 2021 (print) | LCC GV351 (ebook) | DDC
   796.04/3–dc23
LC record available at https://lccn.loc.gov/2019049069
LC ebook record available at https://lccn.loc.gov/2019049070

Printed in the United States of America

Some of the images in this book illustrate individuals who are models. The depictions do not imply actual situations or events.

CPSIA compliance information: Batch #BS20K: For further information contact Greenhaven Publishing LLC, New York, New York at 1-844-317-7404.

Please visit our website, www.greenhavenpublishing.com. For a free color catalog of all our high-quality books, call toll free 1-844-317-7404 or fax 1-844-317-7405.

Find us on

CONTENTS

STUDENT-ATHLETE?

A student-athlete is a student who also plays on one or more of their school's sports teams. Most people use the term "student-athletes" to talk about college students. Many colleges offer **scholarships** for student-athletes, and the students get a lot of other benefits, such as extra help outside of the classroom.

Some people think student-athletes should also be paid money for playing on a sports team. These people say it's a job just like any other. Other people say student-athletes are students first and athletes second, and no other student gets paid to go to school. Understanding both sides of this argument is important so you can have an informed, or educated, opinion.

Know the Facts!

According to the National Collegiate Athletic Association (NCAA), there are more than 460,000 student-athletes in North America.

The NCAA is an **organization** student-athletes belong to. It helps them with things such as getting healthy meals and paying for necessities their scholarship doesn't cover.

Who Gets
PAID?

Not all college sports are popular. Football and basketball are the sports that make schools and the NCAA the most money. Because of that, some people think only college football and basketball players should get paid. Many schools say they would lose money if they had to pay all of their student-athletes.

Others think that's not fair to people who play less popular sports, such as soccer, baseball, and lacrosse. These people say either all student-athletes should be paid or none of them should. They believe it's not fair to pick and choose who gets paid. Student-athletes who don't play football or basketball still work hard and spend a lot of time practicing their sport.

Know the Facts!

March Madness is the name of the NCAA's yearly men's basketball **tournament**. About 100 million people watch it on TV each year.

Some sports are more popular than others. Do you think that should play a part in deciding if all student-athletes should be paid?

Student-Athletes
WORK HARD

People who think student-athletes should be paid point out that playing a sport well is hard work—especially when someone has homework to do! Student-athletes have to go to class, do homework, practice their sport, and take care of themselves. They often don't have time to get a job too.

People who support paying student-athletes say that playing a college sport is the same as having a job. It takes just as much time and hard work. Also, student-athletes are more likely to get hurt than people who don't play a sport. Many people think student-athletes should be paid as a **reward** for their work and for **risking** their health.

Know the Facts!

As of 2017, the highest-level student-athletes spend about 35 hours each week on their sport, including games, practices, and other activities. That's almost as much time as a full-time job!

Students who don't play sports often get a job to help them pay for the things they need. Some people think student-athletes should be paid if they don't have time to get a job.

Too Many BENEFITS

Some people think paying student-athletes would be unfair to other students. They point out that student-athletes already get a lot of benefits that other students don't. Many student-athletes get a scholarship to go to school, but many other students either have to get a job or borrow money to help them pay for school.

A student-athlete's scholarship often includes a small amount of money to help them pay for things they need, such as books. People who don't support paying student-athletes believe this money is part of their reward for playing a sport, so they don't need more.

Know the Facts!

People who borrow money to pay for college have to pay it back. This is called being in debt. According to *Forbes* magazine, in 2019, student debt was the highest it's ever been.

Some people don't think it's fair for student-athletes to finish school with no debt when student debt is a big problem for so many other people.

Making
MONEY

The NCAA makes money by showing college sports on TV, and schools make money by selling tickets to games. College coaches also make a lot of money when their players are successful. Many people think that since student-athletes are making money for other people, they should get some of that money too.

Sometimes other companies also make money from student-athletes. A big company such as Nike might ask a student-athlete to wear something that has its **logo** on it. This is called an endorsement. Until October 2019, the NCAA didn't allow players to get paid for endorsements, even though the companies made money from them.

Know the Facts!

In 2019, California passed a law allowing student-athletes in that state to get paid for endorsements. Soon after that, the NCAA decided to change its rules.

Some student-athletes become very famous. When fans see their favorite players wearing a company's logo, sometimes they want to buy the things that company makes. This is why endorsements are good for a company.

School Isn't About
MONEY

Some people point out that student-athletes are students first and athletes second. College is often seen as a place to prepare for a future job. Playing a school sport teaches student-athletes skills they'll need if they want to become **professional** athletes.

Not all student-athletes want to play sports professionally, though. Some play sports just to help them pay for school through their scholarship. Some people worry that paying student-athletes will make them care less about their classes. If student-athletes don't work hard in school, they'll have a hard time getting a good job after they graduate, or finish school.

Know the Facts!

According to the NCAA, fewer than 2 percent of student-athletes become professional athletes after they graduate. Most get jobs that have to do with the classes they took in school.

Many people believe that college is supposed to be about learning and not about making money. These people worry that student-athletes won't work as hard in school if they're already making money for playing their sport.

Helping with Money
MANAGEMENT

Paying student-athletes is sometimes seen as a good way to help young adults learn how to save money. If a student-athlete becomes a professional athlete, they often suddenly make a lot of money. If they've never earned money for playing their sport before, they might spend too much of it and get into debt.

If student-athletes were paid instead of getting a scholarship, they might learn how to **manage** their money. The schools could help by offering classes in money management. That way, student-athletes would have help from **experts** instead of trying to figure it out on their own.

Know the Facts!

According to the sports TV channel ESPN, about 60 percent of professional basketball players get into debt because of poor money management habits.

Not every student-athlete will make as much money after college as Stephen Curry (shown here). However, everyone needs to learn how to manage their money.

Not Really
HELPING

Most schools don't offer money management classes. Because of this, some people think that giving young adults too much money too soon could actually make them worse at managing money instead of better. If student-athletes were paid instead of getting a scholarship, some say, they might end up spending the money on fun things instead of saving it to pay for school.

People also wonder who would pay student-athletes and where that money would come from. If it's the school, would they raise **tuition** for other students? Many people don't think that's fair to students who don't play a sport.

Know the Facts!

As of 2019, the average tuition at a private college was about $36,800 per year.

Most of the schools with the best sports teams charge a high tuition. If student-athletes got money instead of a scholarship, they might not make enough to pay for their classes at a school such as Duke University.

ARGUMENTS

Most people agree that student-athletes work hard. However, not everyone agrees that this means they should get paid. There are a lot of other things to think about when it comes to whether or not student-athletes should be paid. It's not a simple decision. The most important thing to think about is what's best for the student-athlete—and some people think paying them wouldn't be good for them at all.

Now that you know both sides of the argument, what do you think? Are there more reasons for or against paying student-athletes? Which reasons make the most sense to you?

Know the Facts!

According to the NCAA, 69 percent of people have said they don't think student-athletes should be paid if they also get a scholarship.

Should student-athletes be paid?

YES

- Student-athletes often can't get a job because their sport takes up so much of their time.

- Schools, coaches, and the NCAA make a lot of money, but the players don't get any of it.

- Earning money could help student-athletes learn money management skills early in life.

- Student-athletes put their health at risk to play their sport.

NO

- Student-athletes already get a lot of benefits that other students don't; it would be unfair to give them more.

- Student-athletes are in school to get an education, not to make money.

- Student-athletes might not spend their money the right way or learn to manage it wisely.

- It's hard to figure out a way to pay student-athletes that's fair to everyone and doesn't cost the school more money.

A chart like this one can help you form your opinion about important issues.

GLOSSARY

expert: A person who has special skills or knowledge.

logo: A symbol that is used to identify an organization.

manage: To control or be in charge of something.

organization: A group formed for a specific purpose.

professional: Referring to the job someone does for a living.

reward: Something given to someone to repay them for something they have done.

risk: To put in danger.

scholarship: Money a student gets that is used to help them pay for school.

tournament: A sports competition or series of contests that involves many players or teams and generally continues for several days or weeks.

tuition: Money a school charges students to attend classes.

For More
INFORMATION

WEBSITES

National Collegiate Athletic Association (NCAA)
www.ncaa.org
Learn more about the benefits student-athletes get from the NCAA.

***Vittana*: "14 Should College Athletes Be Paid Pros and Cons"**
vittana.org/14-should-college-athletes-be-paid-pros-and-cons
This article lists seven reasons why student-athletes should be paid and seven reasons why they shouldn't.

BOOKS

Omoth, Tyler. *College Basketball's Championship*. North Mankato, MN: Capstone Press, 2018.

Terp, Gail. *The Debate About Paying College Athletes*. Lake Elmo, MN: Focus Readers, 2018.

Walters, John. *Inside College Football: Preparing for the Pros?*. Broomall, PA: Mason Crest, 2017.

INDEX